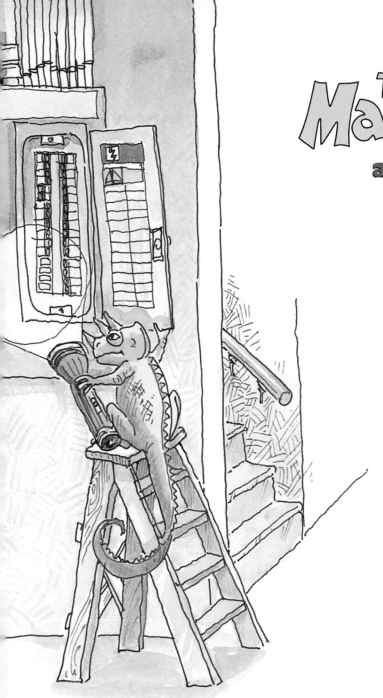

The Magic School Bus

and the Electric Field Trip

The Magic School Bus
and the Electric Field Trip

By Joanna Cole / Illustrated by Bruce Degen

Scholastic Inc.

New York · Toronto · London · Auckland · Sydney
Mexico City · New Delhi · Hong Kong · Buenos Aires

For their careful reading of the manuscript and sketches, we thank Mark Reed, Professor of Electrical Engineering and Applied Physics, and Chairman of Electrical Engineering, Yale University, New Haven, Connecticut; Robert Von Achen, Team Leader, Millstone Information and Science Center; and Michael Templeton, Science Content Director, Magic School Bus television series.

The author thanks Bruce Rideout for lengthy discussions about alternating current, and Vin Licursi for sharing his expertise on electric motors. A big thank you goes to Stephanie Calmenson for her indispensable insights and enthusiasm.

Lauren Thompson, our editor at Scholastic, experimented tirelessly with the mini-generator shown on page 12, and found out that it will not light a light. She also discovered that a moving compass needle does not prove that current is flowing. Michael Templeton helped us decide how to build the final device, for which we are very grateful.

The illustrator thanks Bill Stax, Cheryl Duey, Charlie Chapin, Ray Plue, and Kathy Britt for showing him all about electricity at Connecticut Light and Power.

ISBN-13: 978-0-590-44683-9
ISBN-10: 0-590-44683-5

51 52   19 20 21 22/0

Printed in the U.S.A.   40

The illustrator used pen and ink, watercolor, color pencil,
and gouache for the paintings in this book.

To Rachel—Watt a gal!   **J. C.**

To Trevor and Garrett and all the Roses,
especially Matt, who opened my line
to the electric company.   **B. D.**

Every once in a while, Ms. Frizzle looked out the window and murmured to herself, "She should be here any minute." "*Who* should be here?" we wondered, as we made a list of everything in our classroom that uses electricity.

THESE USE ELECTRICITY:

LIGHTS   COMPUTER
CD and DVD PLAYER
BELL
FAN
CLOCK
TV
BUS BATTERY

THERE'S NO ONE LIKE MS. FRIZZLE.

SHE'S DEFINITELY ONE-OF-A-KIND.

SO IS HER DRESS!

ELECTRICITY ...OUR POWERFUL FRIEND

BE SMART!
BE SAFE!
ELECTRICITY IS USEFUL, BUT IT CAN BE DANGEROUS, TOO. IT CAN HURT YOU... OR EVEN KILL YOU.
BE CAREFUL AROUND ELECTRICITY!

EVERYTHING IS MADE OF ATOMS
by Arnold

The air you are breathing... the book you are reading... the floor under your feet... even your own body — all of these are made of atoms.

ATOMS ARE VERY, VERY, VERY, VERY, VERY SMALL!
by Wanda

It would take more than a million atoms to stretch across the width of just one human hair.

Just then, a red-haired girl cartwheeled into the room. "Hello, Aunt Valerie," said the girl, kissing Ms. Frizzle on the cheek.

"My niece, Dottie Frizzle, is visiting today," said the Friz. "Dottie, we're learning about electricity!"

Dottie seemed excited about science — just like the Friz.

OOOH! I JUST LOVE ELECTRICITY!

FIRST WE HAVE TO LEARN ABOUT ATOMS.

OOOH! I JUST LOVE ATOMS!

Ms. Frizzle took out a pointer and said, "Class, to understand electricity, we must understand atoms. Here is a giant model of an atom."
She pointed to the outer part of the atom model.
"These tiny parts of the atom are called electrons," she said.

ELECTRONS MOVE AROUND THE NUCLEUS --OR CENTER-- OF THE ATOM.

OOOH! I LOVE ELECTRONS!

Electron

Electron

Nucleus

THE ATOM

TWO FRIZZLES!? IT JUST ISN'T FAIR!

"Most of the time, electrons stay with their own atom," continued the Friz.
"But sometimes electrons get pulled away.
They leave one atom and jump to the next.
They make a stream that runs from atom to atom.
This stream is called electric current."

Outside, the sky got darker and darker by the minute, and big raindrops started plopping down.
Ms. Frizzle picked up a roll of electrical wire.
"I am peeling off some of the plastic insulation to show you the copper wire inside," she said.

THE METAL WIRE MAKES A PATH FOR THE ELECTRONS. THE PLASTIC COVERING KEEPS THEM IN THE WIRE-- AND AWAY FROM US.

WOW! IT'S A SUPER-HIGHWAY FOR ELECTRONS!

SOME MATERIALS ARE GOOD PATHS
by Carlos
Current runs through some materials easily. Why? Because their electrons are loosely bound. They travel easily from atom to atom.

Some good paths:
Metals   Acids
    Water

OTHER MATERIALS ARE GOOD BLOCKERS

In some other materials the electrons are tightly bound. It's hard for them to run.
    Good blockers make good insulators.

Some good blockers:
Plastic   Rubber
Wood   Glass   Air

MAKING A MINI-POWER PLANT
by Ralphie

What we use:
-- 6 feet of thin copper wire
-- Bar magnet
-- Meter to measure current

What we do:
-- Wrap wire into coil (400 turns)
-- Attach wire ends to meter
-- Move magnet inside coil

Meter →

Magnet ↓

← Wire

What happens:
-- The meter needle moves!

Why it happens:
-- Moving the magnet makes current flow in the wire.
-- Current makes the needle move.

ELECTRICITY HAS A SPECIAL RELATIONSHIP WITH MAGNETISM.

Magnetism can make electricity.

Frizzie said that one way to make electric current is to move a magnet near a wire.
We made a tiny power plant in our classroom.
We were making electric current!
Our mini-power plant can move one little needle.
But the city power plant sends enough electricity for our whole town.

YOU MEAN JUST MOVING A MAGNET NEAR A WIRE MAKES ELECTRONS TRAVEL?

YES, RALPHIE, BUT WE MUST HAVE AN UNBROKEN CIRCUIT --CIRCLE--OF WIRE.

IF THE CIRCUIT IS BROKEN, THE NEEDLE WON'T MOVE.

Just then, lightning flashed and thunder cracked outside.
The lights in our room flickered and went out.
All the appliances stopped running.
"There's no electricity!" someone yelped.
"We're experiencing a blackout," said the Friz.
"Let's find out what happened."

Q: WHAT IS LIGHTNING?
A: IT IS ELECTRICITY!
      by Phoebe
When a storm happens, extra electrons stick to tiny drops of water or ice.
   When enough of them gather together in one place, they jump.
   This is a bolt of lightning!

LIGHTNING SAFETY RULES
DURING A LIGHTNING STORM:
--DO NOT STAY OUTDOORS.
   GO INTO A HOUSE, CAR, OR BUS.
--DO NOT USE THE TELEPHONE.
--DO NOT USE ELECTRIC APPLIANCES.
--DO NOT GO NEAR WATER.

Soon we were riding on the old school bus, trying to find out what had caused the blackout. It wasn't long before we saw the problem. The lightning had hit a tree and knocked it down. The falling tree had broken a power line. Sparks were flying everywhere.

ELECTRONS CAN'T RUN TO OUR SCHOOL BECAUSE THE PATHWAY IS BROKEN.

WHERE ARE THOSE ELECTRONS WHEN YOU NEED THEM?

WOW!

"Help! Let's get out of here!" we yelled.
The Friz didn't waste a minute.
She made a U-turn and drove away.

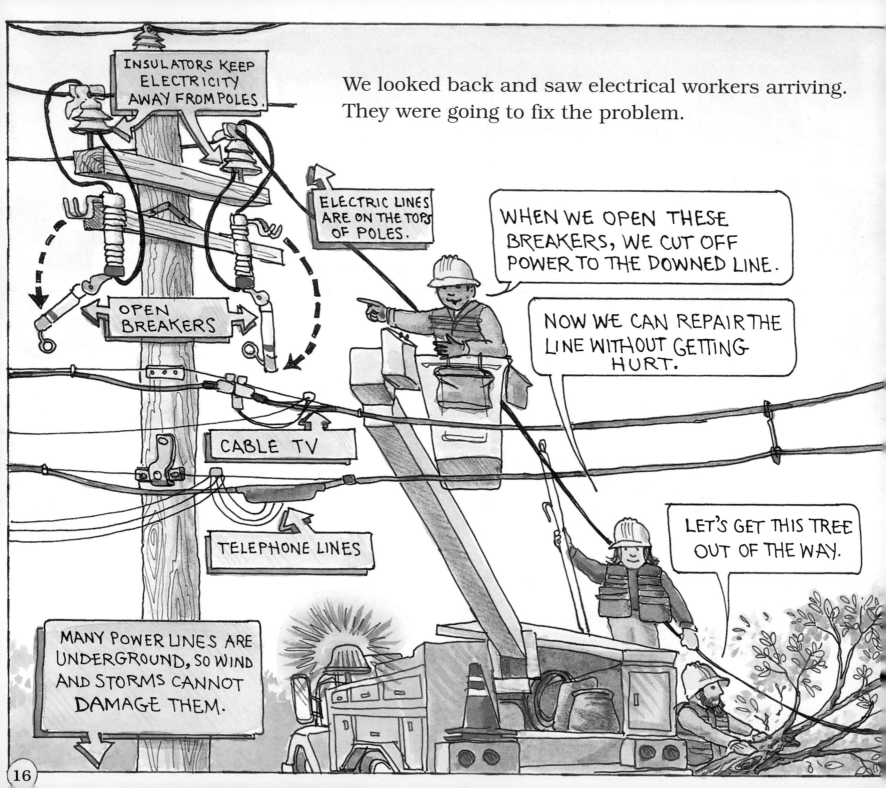

We looked back and saw electrical workers arriving. They were going to fix the problem.

Up ahead was the town's power plant.
It looked like a little city of buildings.
"Inside those buildings is the equipment that makes electricity, class," Ms. Frizzle told us.
"Oooh, let's visit the power plant now," suggested Ms. Frizzle's niece.
"What a wonderful idea, Dottie!" crowed the Friz.
"Hang on, everyone!"

WHEN I GROW UP I WANT TO BE JUST LIKE MY AUNT VAL.

DON'T WORRY --YOU ALREADY ARE!

HOW WE FIX A BROKEN LINE

① AFTER WE ARE SURE ALL THE BREAKERS ARE OPEN, WE CAN BEGIN WORK.

② THEN WE PULL THE BROKEN ENDS TOGETHER.

ROPE AND PULLEYS

③ NEXT WE SPLICE THE WIRES TOGETHER.

SPLICER IS LIKE THE FINGER TOY ~ THE MORE YOU PULL OUTWARD THE TIGHTER IT HOLDS THE FINGERS.

④ WE PUT THE LINE BACK UP.

⑤ WE CLOSE THE BREAKERS AGAIN.

⑥ WE'RE DONE! ON TO THE NEXT JOB.

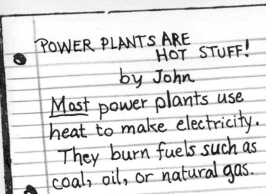

POWER PLANTS ARE HOT STUFF!
by John

Most power plants use heat to make electricity. They burn fuels such as coal, oil, or natural gas.

THE GOOD NEWS:
Fuel-burning plants can make huge amounts of power.

THE BAD NEWS:
They all make air pollution.

Some plants get heat from nuclear reactors.

THE GOOD NEWS:
These make huge amounts of power without air pollution.

THE BAD NEWS:
They create nuclear wastes.

When we arrived at the plant, Ms. Frizzle gave us heat-proof suits and said, "We'll begin our tour by observing the fuel supply." She pushed a little button on the dashboard, and the bus changed into a dump truck. "Making a delivery!" Ms. Frizzle yelled.

The dump truck tipped up, and
we went tumbling down the coal chute.
We landed in the coal bin and slid
right into a furnace of flames.
"Let's see what all this heat is used for,"
said Ms. Frizzle.

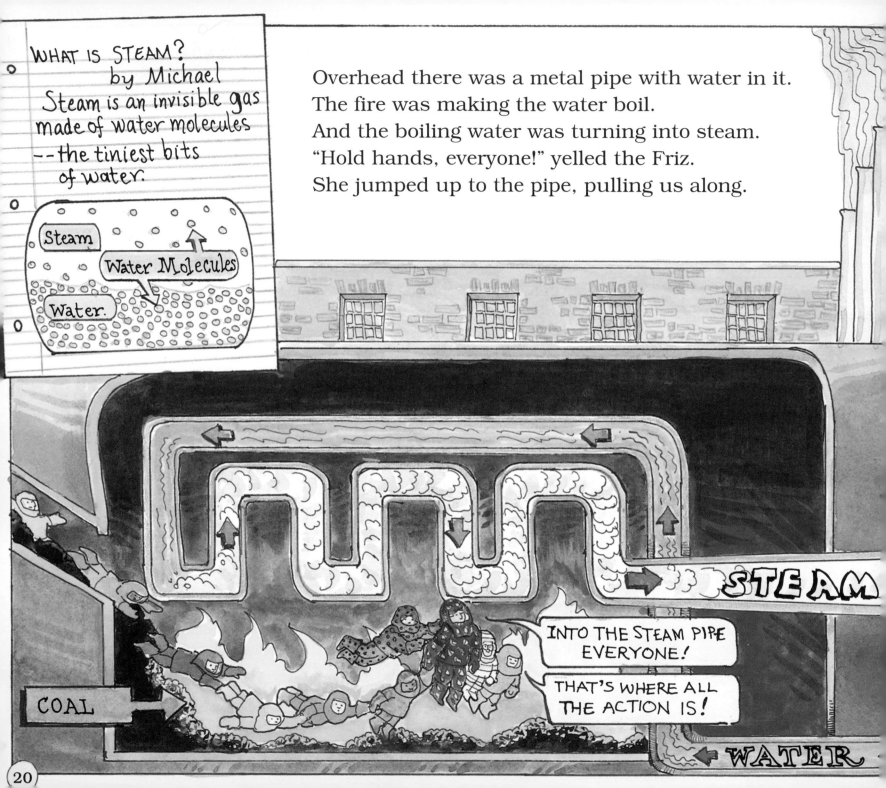

In a second, our whole class was inside the steam pipe. The steam was traveling at high speed — and we were, too. "Now we'll learn what all this steam is used for, class," called Ms. Frizzle. We steamed along through the pipe and into the next room in the power plant.

STEAM CAN DO WORK
by Shirley
When steam is heated in a closed container it pushes out.
We can use this pressure to do jobs for us.

WA-HOO! FULL STEAM AHEAD!

THE STEAM IN THIS POT HAS "PUSH" POWER.

IT'S PUSHING UP THE LID.

THIS STEAM IS UNDER HIGH PRESSURE, CLASS.

I'VE NEVER BEEN COMFORTABLE IN HIGH-PRESSURE SITUATIONS.

Steam Pipe
Boiler
Turbine
Generator
Where we are in the power plant

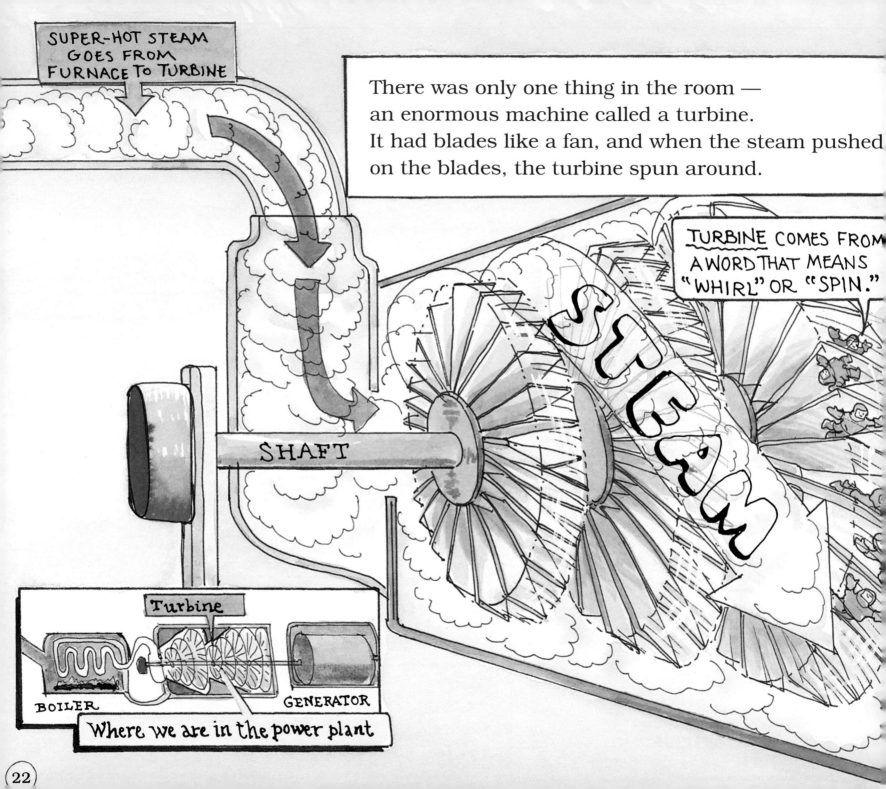

SUPER-HOT STEAM GOES FROM FURNACE TO TURBINE

There was only one thing in the room —
an enormous machine called a turbine.
It had blades like a fan, and when the steam pushed
on the blades, the turbine spun around.

TURBINE COMES FROM A WORD THAT MEANS "WHIRL" OR "SPIN."

STEAM

SHAFT

BOILER

Turbine

GENERATOR

Where we are in the power plant

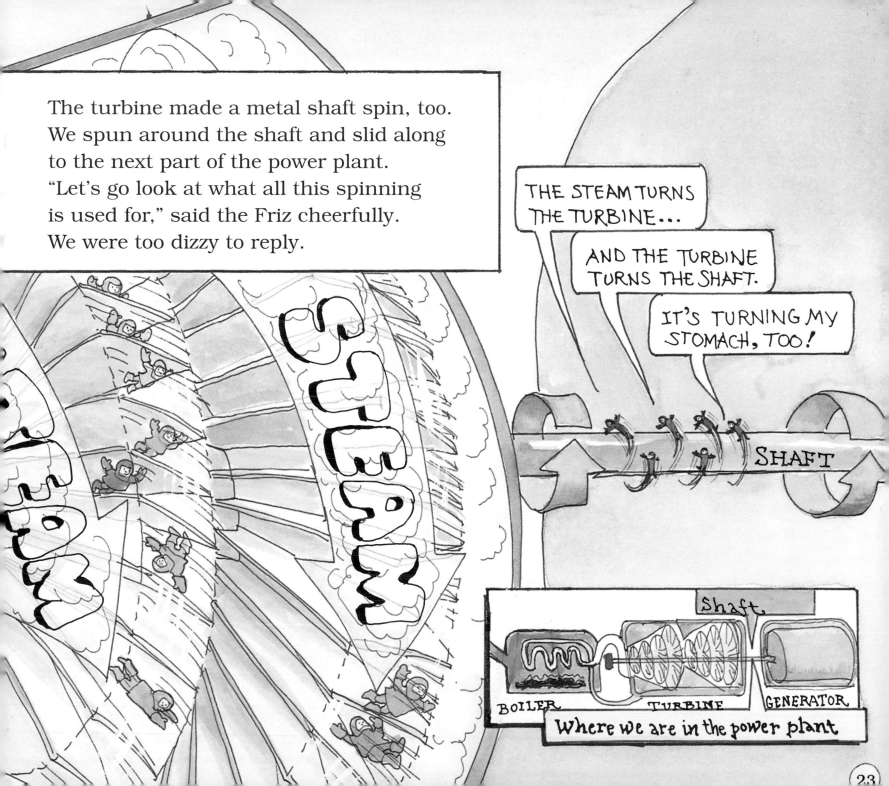

The turbine made a metal shaft spin, too.
We spun around the shaft and slid along
to the next part of the power plant.
"Let's go look at what all this spinning
is used for," said the Friz cheerfully.
We were too dizzy to reply.

THE STEAM TURNS THE TURBINE...

AND THE TURBINE TURNS THE SHAFT.

IT'S TURNING MY STOMACH, TOO!

SHAFT

Shaft

BOILER   TURBINE   GENERATOR

Where we are in the power plant

23

Then the current flowed into a power line or large wire leading out of the plant. "Next we'll observe what all this electricity is used for," said the Friz.
Suddenly we began to get smaller... and smaller... and smaller... until we could fit inside the power line.

CLASS, WE ARE LEAVING THE POWER PLANT BY HIGH-VOLTAGE WIRE!

OOOH! I LOVE HIGH VOLTAGE!

I'VE ALWAYS THOUGHT OF MYSELF AS A LOW-VOLTAGE KIND OF PERSON...

WHAT ARE VOLTS?
    by Rachel
Volts measure the "push" of electric current.
The higher the voltage, the more pressure there is to push the current through the wire.

CURRENT LEAVES POWER PLANT AT 24,000 VOLTS

On the way, we passed through transformers, devices that made the voltage in the wire higher or lower. Higher voltage helps the current travel the long distance from the plant to the places that will use the electricity. Lower voltages are used in factories and big businesses. Still lower voltages are used in small buildings and homes.
"Where are we going?" someone asked.
"We're on our way to a lightbulb," the Friz answered calmly.

WHY IS MS. FRIZZLE TAKING US TO A LIGHTBULB?

BECAUSE SHE DOESN'T WANT TO GO TO A HEAVY BULB.

GET IT?

DO ELECTRONS RUN ONLY ONE WAY IN THE POWER LINE?
by Arnold
No! The electric current in the power line changes direction many times every second.
This is called alternating current or "ac" for short.

A WORD FROM DOROTHY ANN
Transform means to "change."
A transformer changes the voltage from high to low, or from low to high.

Down to 13,800 volts

Down to 110 or 220 volts

TRANSFORMER lowers the voltage for use in factories and large businesses

TRANSFORMER lowers the voltage for use in homes

A WORD FROM DOROTHY ANN

Filament comes from a word that means "thread." The first filaments were made of burnt cotton thread or even bamboo.

First Bulbs

Cotton

Bamboo

Today's filaments are made of a strong metal called tungsten.

BE SMART!
BE SAFE!
DON'T PUT YOUR FINGERS, YOUR TAIL, OR ANYTHING ELSE IN AN ELECTRIC OUTLET!

We were moving down the power line when Ms. Frizzle said, "Here we are at the town library." We followed her through the wires and into a lamp. "We're going right into the lightbulb!" Wanda cried. Inside the bulb, we squeezed into a very, very, very thin wire — the filament. "The filament makes the bulb light up," said Ms. Frizzle

FILAMENT
CONNECTING WIRES
BASE

BULB

HEY, THERE'S MY MOM. SHE'S CHECKING OUT BOOKS FOR ME.

OOOH! THIS TIN' FILAMENT MAKE A BIG LIGHT!

Billions and billions of electrons were pushing
through the thin filament all at once.
That made the filament get white hot.
When something is white hot, it glows with light.
We scarcely had time to put on our sunglasses
before we were in and out of the bulb.
Then we were heading away from the library.
We didn't even have a chance to check out any books!

A HEATING ELEMENT IS LIKE THE FILAMENT IN A LIGHTBULB-- IT MAKES HEAT AND LIGHT.

BUT IT MAKES MORE HEAT THAN LIGHT.

We traveled down the street through the power line until we came to Jo's Diner.
Once inside the restaurant, we entered a toaster.
"Now we'll observe how electricity makes heat," said the Friz.
"Follow me into the heating element!"
The heating element was a coil made of a special kind of wire.
When electricity flowed through the wire, it got red hot!

PHEW--IT'S WARM TODAY!

YOU THINK YOU'RE WARM-- YOU SHOULD BE IN THE KITCHEN!

YOU THINK YOU'RE WARM--YOU SHOULD BE IN THE TOASTER!

The heating element was making some toast.
That reminded us — wasn't it almost lunchtime?
Ms. Frizzle didn't stop. Maybe she wasn't hungry.
She went out the wire to the main power line again.
"We will now visit someone's house," she said,
making a sharp turn.
"I wonder whose house," murmured Phoebe.

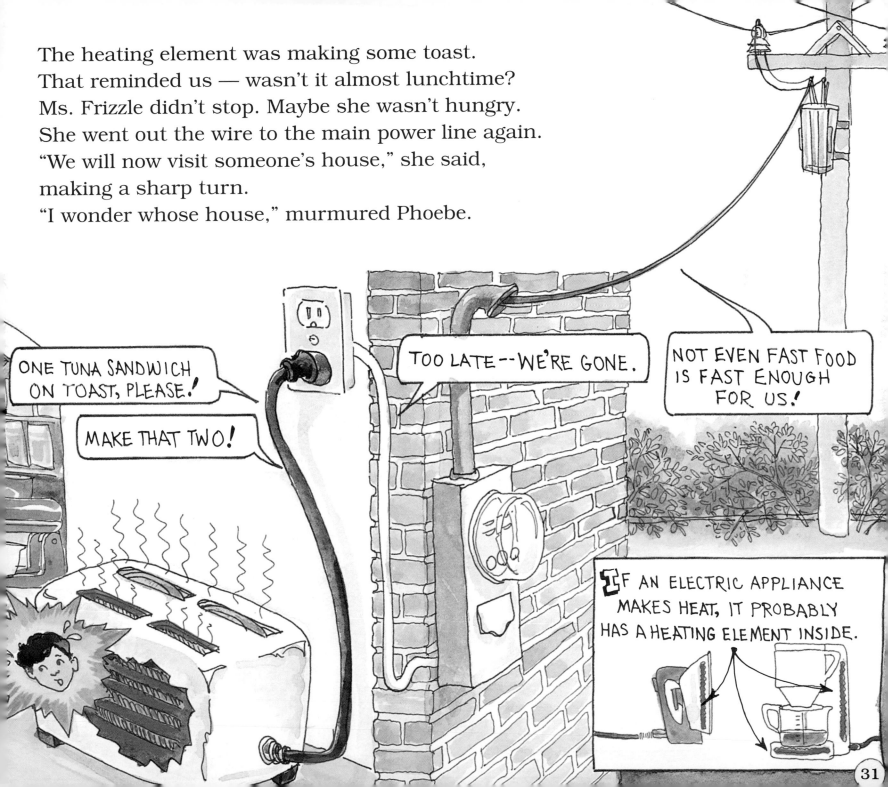

ONE TUNA SANDWICH ON TOAST, PLEASE!

MAKE THAT TWO!

TOO LATE -- WE'RE GONE.

NOT EVEN FAST FOOD IS FAST ENOUGH FOR US!

IF AN ELECTRIC APPLIANCE MAKES HEAT, IT PROBABLY HAS A HEATING ELEMENT INSIDE.

It was Phoebe's house!
Her grandma was using a power saw
to make a bookcase for Phoebe's room.
"Oh good," said Ms. Frizzle. "This gives us a chance
to see how the saw is driven by an electric motor."
Ms. Frizzle said an electric motor has magnets inside.

I HOPE PHOEBE LIKES THIS.

WELCOME HOME, PHOEBE.

AT MY OLD SCHOOL
I NEVER CAME HOME
IN THE MIDDLE OF
THE DAY.

"Remember how we made electric current with a magnet?" asked Frizzie. "Well, it works the other way, too. Electric current can turn a piece of metal into a magnet. This kind of magnet is called an electromagnet. Electromagnets are what make the motor run."

If an electric appliance has moving parts...

It probably has a motor.

"Now for a tour of the electric motor,"
called Ms. Frizzle.
We ran through the wire and into the motor.
Everything was whirring and shaking in there.

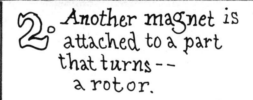

Motor comes from a word that means "to move."

This is a very moving experience

HOW A MOTOR WORKS

Inside a motor, electromagnets make a moving part spin.

1. An electromagnet is attached to a part of the motor that does not move-- the stator.

2. Another magnet is attached to a part that turns -- a rotor.

3. The stator magnet's north pole pulls on the rotor magnet's south pole. This makes the rotor turn.

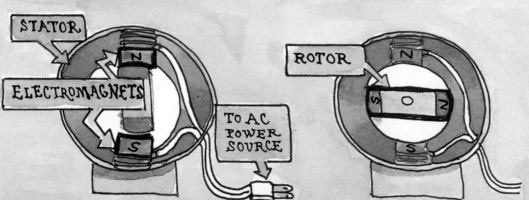

STATOR

ELECTROMAGNETS

TO AC POWER SOURCE

ROTOR

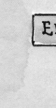

A cylinder called a rotor was turning very fast.
The rotor was attached to a shaft, and the shaft
was attached to the saw blade.
The spinning rotor made the blade turn
so it could cut wood.

STATOR

ROTOR

SAW BLADE

4. Then the alternating current in the wire coil changes direction. This makes the poles of the stator magnet switch places.

5. Now the electromagnet's south pole is next to the rotor magnet's south pole. These poles are the same, so they push each other away. This makes the rotor turn away from the electromagnet's south pole.

6. The current keeps alternating, so the rotor keeps turning.

THESE DIAGRAMS ARE TOO HARD FOR ME.

Poles switch

Poles switch again

I'M GOING TO STUDY THEM LATER...

MUCH LATER!

While we were in the motor, Phoebe's grandma kept sawing.
She didn't notice the cat creeping up on the bird cage.
"Watch out!" squawked the parrot.
But it was too late. The cage fell over, scattering
bird seed and other stuff all over the carpet.
Phoebe's grandpa came to the rescue
with the vacuum cleaner.

"Come on, kids!" called Ms. Frizzle. "We have to see this!"
She led us out of the power saw, in one outlet,
through the wires in the walls, out another outlet,
and into the vacuum cleaner wire.

THE MOTOR IN THE VACUUM CLEANER WORKS
JUST LIKE THE ONE IN THE POWER SAW.

EXCEPT THAT INSTEAD OF MOVING A
SAW BLADE THIS MOTOR TURNS A FAN.

I GET IT-- THE FAN SUCKS AIR INTO THE CLEANER.

AND WHEN THE AIR GOES IN--
THE DIRT GOES WITH IT.

WELL I'M NOT GOING IN!

Exhaust air

BAG

DIRT

AIR & DIRT

SUCTION FAN

BRUSH

MOTOR

SHAFT

AIR AND DIRT

HOW A SWITCH WORKS
by Alex

Inside the appliance, the wires are connected by two metal pieces called contacts.

Switch On	Switch Off
CONTACTS TOUCH	GAP

TURNING IT ON

When you switch to "ON," the switch pulls the contacts together. They make a little bridge between the wires. Then electrons can flow and the appliance works.

TURNING IT OFF

When you switch to "OFF," the switch pulls the metal pieces apart. The electrons cannot flow, and the appliance shuts down.

We were getting ready to leave, when Grandpa finished vacuuming and turned off the switch. That made a gap in the electric pathway. No more electrons could flow past the gap, so the motor stopped running.

IT'S TIME TO GO.

FORGET IT -- NO ONE IS GOING ANYWHERE.

NOT EVEN MS. FRIZZLE.

NOW THAT'S A SWITCH!

DOES A LIGHT SWITCH WORK LIKE THIS, TOO?

YES, ALL SWITCHES DO.

CONTACT

GAP

CONTACT

We called to Grandpa, but he couldn't hear us. Phoebe was worried. She had to get back in time for an after-school karate class. The rest of us were playing in a soccer game. But what could we do? We were stuck in the switch of a vacuum cleaner!

SAVE US, GRANDPA!

FORGET IT—— HE'S WATCHING TV.

AT LEAST IT'S SOMETHING EDUCATIONAL!

DIRT EATER

1. TV signals are sent by the TV station.

2. The signals cause tiny electric currents in your antenna or cable.

3. The little currents control an electron gun in the picture tube in your TV.

Red
Blue
Green

4. The electron gun shoots electrons at the back of your TV screen.

5. The screen is coated with thousands of dots made of phosphor —— a chemical.

6. When electrons hit the phosphor dots, the dots glow with light.

7. The phosphor dots form shapes on the screen.

GET THE PICTURE?

Suddenly we heard loud barking.
Phoebe's puppy had been digging holes in the garden.
He came inside, all covered with dirt.
The first thing he did was to roll around on the carpet.

Grandpa had to switch on the vacuum cleaner again.
The switch pulled the contacts together,
and the electric path was complete again.
"Follow me back to school, kids,"
yelled Ms. Frizzle.
We went through the switch, out the wire,
to the outside power lines, down the street,
and into the wires in the school's walls.

We flowed through an outlet and into the wire
of a floor waxing machine.
The next thing we knew we were
popping out of a hole in the wire's insulation.

As soon as we had grown to our regular size,
Ms. Frizzle led us back to the classroom.

It had been *some* day!
We'd gone through fires and wires.
We'd had close encounters with subatomic particles.
And we'd seen a new side of home appliances — the inside.

Now everything was back to normal in our class.
Well… everything except Ms. Frizzle, of course!

LOOK AT HER DRESS!

UH-OH! I SENSE TROUBLE.

...ANT

...THAT MADE ...ELECTRICITY!

...ECTRI-SILLY—

SPRING BULBS by Carlos

Tough Assignment—Due Tomorrow

HOW DO THESE ELECTRIC APPLIANCES WORK?

choose the correct answer

IRON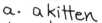

To make heat, it has:
a. a kitten
b. a heating element
c. wool socks

POWER DRILL

To move the drill bit, it has:
a. a motor
b. a rubber band
c. a rubber duck

HAIR DRYER

It makes heat _and_ has a moving part--a fan to blow air--so it needs:
a. a heating element and a pickle
b. a pickle and a motor
c. a heating element and a motor.

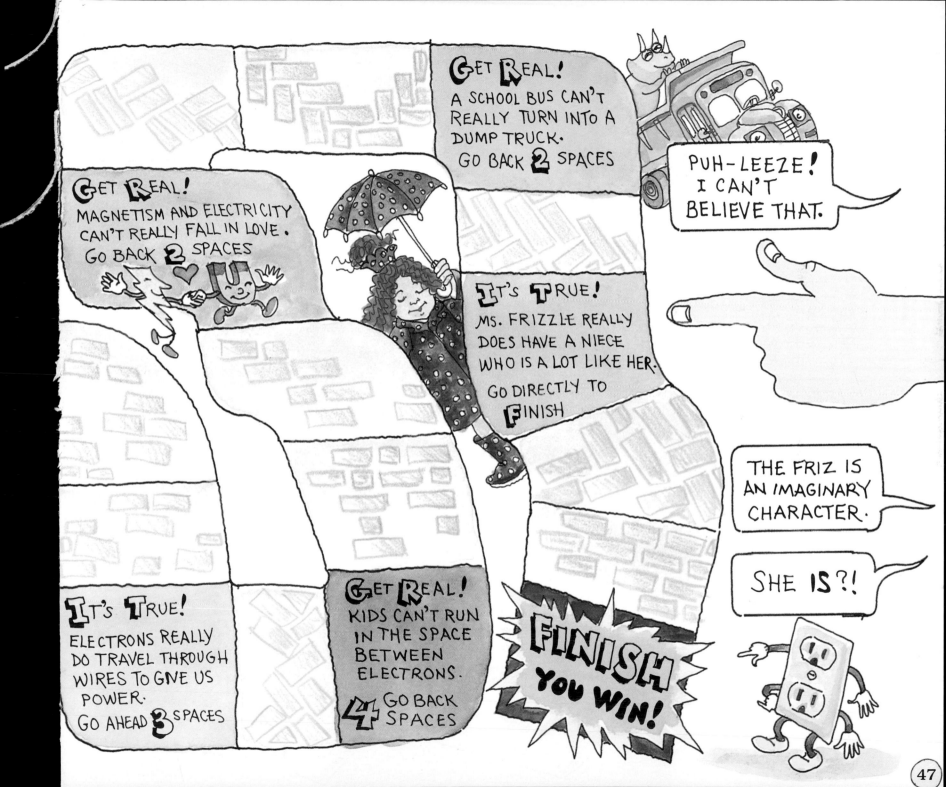